Fire in the Pulpit

An Urgent Call for Transformation

Charles E. Cravey

In His Steps Publishing Company

ISBN: 978-1-58535-109-1 (Paperback)

ISBN: 978-1-58535-110-7 (Kindle)

Library of Congress Catalog Number: 2025915976

Cover Design by Book Brush and Charles E. Cravey

Printed in the United States of America.

Published by In His Steps Publishing, Statesboro, Georgia.

Contents

Dedication:

To the pulpiteers whose voices may tremble but never fade—
who see the pulpit not as platform, but as an altar,
And preach not for applause, but for awakening.

To the saints in the pews who pray with fire,
who long not for spectacle, but for Spirit,
and who believe that revival still breathes in whisper and wind.

To you, dear reader—
may this book stir what was sleeping,
rekindle what was sacred,
and send forth embers of truth
into every heart longing to burn again.

FIRE IN THE PULPIT

Preface

When the Alarms Ring in Heaven

There are moments in history when the Church must not simply gather—it must awaken. This book was born from one such moment.

As a pastor, storyteller, theologian, and keeper of legacy, I have watched the pulpit flicker when it should flame. I've seen the slow smolder of complacency, the sparks of division, and the embers of hope buried beneath cultural ash. *FIRE IN THE PULPIT: AN URGENT CALL FOR TRANSFORMATION* is not a diagnosis—**it's a call**. A siren cry from the watchtower of faith.

The five-alarm framework came not from mere metaphor but from meditation. Each "alarm" is a fire signal increasing danger—an escalation of urgency. So too in the Church. What begins as apathy can become a catastrophe if we do not respond with revival.

These pages are not simply mine—they belong to every preacher, worshiper, leader, and seeker who refuses to let the gospel grow cold. They are soaked in prayer, in scripture, in pastoral anguish, and in holy hope.

Let every chapter be a flare. Let every word be kindling. Let this book stir—not just thinking—but transformation.

CHARLES E. CRAVEY
Statesboro, Georgia

Chapter One

Fire in the Pulpit!

There's a Fire in the Pulpit today in a broad range of churches. This metaphorical blaze is not one of destruction but of renewal and passion, as leaders and congregations alike strive to awaken a deeper connection to their faith and mission. This resurgence is fueled by a collective desire to address the growing concerns of spiritual apathy and to reignite the fervor that once defined their communities.

A Personal Anecdote:

"I remember one Sunday in the early stretch of my ministry. I stood behind a humble wooden pulpit in a country church so quiet I could

hear the wind brushing against the stained glass. I felt unprepared, unsure. But as I opened my Bible, my hands trembled—not from fear, but from presence. That day, the Spirit moved not through polished delivery, but through cracked vessels willing to pour. I didn't just preach—I was caught ablaze."

Across denominations, clergy are stepping forward with renewed vigor, delivering sermons that challenge complacency and inspire action. Their messages are infused with a sense of urgency, calling believers to embrace their spiritual journey with enthusiasm and dedication. This revitalized preaching seeks to not only educate but also to motivate, encouraging congregants to live out their faith in tangible and transformative ways.

In tandem with these vibrant sermons, churches are implementing innovative programs and initiatives designed to engage members at all stages of their spiritual journey. From dynamic worship experiences to interactive Bible studies and outreach projects, these efforts aim to create a more inclusive and active faith environment. By fostering a sense of belonging and purpose, churches are empowering individuals to grow spiritually while contributing positively to their communities.

This fire in the pulpit is a testament to the enduring power of faith and the relentless pursuit of spiritual renewal. It serves as a beacon of hope, reminding us that no matter the challenges we face, there is always potential for revival and growth. As congregations come together to fan the flames of their collective passion, they illuminate a path toward a vibrant future, one that is rich with love, purpose, and unwavering commitment to the teachings of Christ.

I will attempt to walk you through the fires that besiege the churches today using the metaphor of the categories of fire that fire departments use to identify how severe and intense a fire is at a specific location, a five-alarm being the most involved and severe.

As we embark on this journey, each "alarm" represents a different level of urgency and intensity within our spiritual communities. By drawing on this metaphor, we will explore the challenges and opportunities at each stage, offering guidance and strategies to address the issues that threaten to dampen the vibrant spirit of our faith communities.

One-Alarm Fire—The Ignition of Apathy: This is where it all begins, with subtle signs of indifference creeping into the congregation. It's the slow burn of disengagement that often goes unnoticed until it starts to affect the broader community. At this stage, awareness is key. We must first recognize the signs of spiritual lethargy and take proactive steps to rekindle enthusiasm and commitment.

Two-Alarm Fire—The Spread of Complacency: As apathy takes root, it can quickly spread into complacency, where the passion for worship and community involvement begins to wane. Here, we need to stoke the flames of interest and involvement by fostering environments that encourage active participation and personal growth. This might involve introducing innovative programs, creating opportunities for deeper engagement, or revitalizing existing traditions to make them more relevant.

Three-Alarm Fire—The Threat of Division: At this level, complacency can lead to division within the church, as differing opinions and lack of enthusiasm create rifts. To combat this, we must focus on unity and reconciliation, emphasizing the common goals and shared values that bind us together. Open dialogue, mutual respect, and collaborative efforts are essential to bridge gaps and heal divisions.

Four-Alarm Fire—The Erosion of Purpose: With division, the church's mission can become obscured, leading to an erosion of purpose. It is crucial to revisit and rearticulate the church's vision, reminding everyone of the core mission and the role they play in fulfilling it. By aligning activities and initiatives with this renewed sense of purpose, we can refocus our efforts and reinvigorate our collective passion.

Five-Alarm Fire—The Crisis of Faith: At its most severe, a crisis of faith can emerge, threatening the very foundation of the community. This is a time for deep reflection and earnest prayer, seeking divine guidance and strength to navigate through the challenges. It requires bold leadership and a willingness to confront difficult truths, all while maintaining an unwavering commitment to healing and renewal.

A Personal Anecdote:
"One morning, I arrived early to prepare the sanctuary. Every-

thing was immaculate—bulletins folded, candles trimmed, pews waiting. Yet as I sat in the silence, I realized something was missing. The room was ready. The people would arrive. But the spiritual fire hadn't been invited. Beauty without presence is simply staging. I learned that day that a pulpit can be perfectly arranged—and still cold to the touch."

Throughout this exploration, we will delve into practical strategies tailored to each stage of the metaphorical fire, equipping you with the tools necessary to not only manage but extinguish these flames. Together, let us strive to transform these challenges into opportunities for growth, emerging stronger and more unified in our faith and purpose.

If you have concerns about your specific church or churches in general, this book is tailored for you. It is crafted with empathy and thoughtfulness, offering genuine, practical solutions for members in today's context.

By addressing the complexities and challenges faced by modern congregations, this book seeks to equip you with the tools necessary to foster a thriving spiritual community. Whether you are a leader striving to inspire your congregation or a member seeking deeper engagement, the insights and strategies presented here are designed to resonate with your unique journey and aspirations.

A Personal Anecdote:

"A young man, not yet twenty, came to me after a sermon and asked, 'Why does the Church seem scared to speak plainly anymore?' His question was sincere, unarmed by cynicism. It ignited something deep in me—a realization that spiritual leadership must reclaim its boldness. It wasn't just a question. It was an alarm bell."

Each chapter builds upon the metaphor of fire, guiding you through the various stages of spiritual renewal and offering actionable steps to reignite the passion within your church. From confronting apathy to embracing unity and purpose, this book provides a roadmap for cultivating a vibrant faith community that is grounded in love and dedicated to growth.

At its core, this book is a celebration of the transformative power of faith and the unwavering hope that lies within each of us. It acknowledges the struggles we face and the resilience required to overcome them, encouraging us to embark on a journey of renewal with open hearts and steadfast determination. Through the shared wisdom and experiences contained within these pages, you are invited to become an active participant in the revitalization of your church, contributing to a legacy of faith that inspires and uplifts all who encounter it.

Let this book be a companion on your spiritual journey, a source of encouragement and inspiration as you navigate the complexities of modern church life. Together, we can illuminate a path toward a future rich with purpose and possibility, where every member is empowered to live out their faith with authenticity and joy.

A SONNET FOR THE CHURCH TODAY

Charles E. Cravey

In hallowed halls where whispers softly tread,
The echoes of our past begin to rise.
A yearning stirs within each heart and head,
To see our faith anew through opened eyes.

With steadfast hope, we seek a brighter dawn.
Where love and grace illuminate the way.
Through trials faced, our spirit carries on.
In unity, we find the strength to pray.

Though shadows may attempt to cloud our view,
We stand as one; our hearts with fervor burn.
In every act of kindness, faith we renew.
To Christ, our eyes and souls will always turn.

O Church, a beacon shining in the night,
Guide us with truth and fill our world with light.

Chapter Two

One-Alarm Fire

The Ignition of Apathy

SONNET FOR A ONE-ALARM FIRE

Charles E. Cravey

Beneath the midnight's cloak, a spark ignites,

A gentle glow against the shadowed night.

It whispers through the silence, softly fights,

Transforming darkness with its fleeting light.

The ember dances to a rhythmic beat,

Its warmth a gentle kiss upon the air.

The world around recoils from such a heat,

Yet drawn to watch, they cannot help but stare.

A single flame, its presence not in vain,

For in its heart lies both the fear and thrill.

A beauty in destruction, not in pain,

A force to fuel the dreams it seeks to fill.

Though small, its power lingers in the soul,

A one-alarm fire, both quiet and whole.

A Personal Anecdote:

"There was a Sunday not long ago when I stood at the entrance of the church, watching people quietly file in—good people, kind people. Yet something felt missing. Smiles were polite but not radiant. Worship songs echoed but didn't soar. In that moment, I didn't feel

discouraged—I felt convicted. Somewhere along the way, we had traded passion for predictability. That morning taught me that spiritual apathy rarely screams—it whispers in the routine."

Let's tackle the first alarm raised in our churches: ***spiritual apathy***. Just as a small spark can ignite a fire, so can the indifference of the members lead to a slow burn of disinterest and disengagement from the faith community. This phenomenon, often insidious in its approach, can gradually deplete the vibrant energy and passion of fervent believers, ultimately leaving them quietly resigned and uninspired.

To begin our exploration, we will delve into the biblical admonition present in **Revelation 2:4**, which addresses the church in Ephesus and criticizes its departure from its initial devotion and fervent love. This scriptural passage powerfully summons us to make an honest evaluation of the depth and intensity of our commitment and devotion to Christ.

A Personal Anecdote:
"An elder once sat across from me after service and said, 'Pastor, I

*remember when we used to cry during altar calls—not from sad-
ness, but because we felt heaven was so close.' His voice cracked, not
from criticism but longing. We sat in silence, listening to our shared
ache. That conversation reminded me that sometimes, apathy isn't
rebellion—it's absence. The absence of awe."*

Upon our initial encounter with the Gospel, a passionate yearning ignites within us—a yearning not only to understand God
deeply but also to immerse ourselves in His divine word and
enthusiastically spread His boundless love among our fellow human beings. However, as time marches relentlessly onward, the
allure of life's myriad distractions and the crushing weight of
daily routine often diminish and obscure that initial, vibrant
passion.

We must strive to reignite that fervor, recognizing that the journey of faith is not meant to be static but dynamic, ever-evolving
as we grow in understanding and love. The admonition in Revelation serves as a gentle reminder to return to our first love, to
recapture the essence of our spiritual beginnings, and to bring
that enthusiasm into our present lives.

In doing so, we are encouraged to engage in practices that nurture our spiritual well-being. This might involve setting aside dedicated time for personal reflection and prayer, allowing ourselves to be still in the presence of God and to listen for His guidance. It's about carving out space in our busy lives for intentional worship, where our focus is wholly on connecting with the divine and expressing our gratitude and devotion.

Moreover, reconnecting with our community can be immensely beneficial. By sharing our experiences and listening to the journeys of others, we gain fresh perspectives and renewed inspiration. This communal support system acts as a catalyst for spiritual rejuvenation, reminding us that we are not alone on this path.

Ultimately, *the call to rekindle our spiritual passion is a call to live authentically and passionately, embracing the fullness of our faith.* It's an invitation to let our lives be a testament to the transformative power of love and devotion, shining brightly in a world that desperately needs hope and light. As we embark on this journey of rediscovery, let us do so with joy and anticipation, knowing that each step brings us closer to a deeper and more fulfilling relationship with God.

In order to fight against the decrease in spirituality, we are going to provide you with some practical steps that you can take to rekindle your spiritual flame and reignite your passion for the spiritual life. Among these are:

- **<u>Daily Devotionals</u>**: Start each day with a moment of quiet reflection. Choose a devotional guide or scripture passage to meditate on, allowing it to set the tone for your day. This practice nurtures a habit of mindfulness and aligns your thoughts with spiritual truths.

- **<u>Intentional Prayer</u>**: Set aside dedicated time for prayer, not just as a routine, but as a heartfelt conversation with God. Share your joys, concerns, and gratitude, and be open to listening for His guidance.

- **<u>Engage in Worship</u>**: Explore different forms of worship that resonate with you, whether it's through music, art, or nature. Attend services with a focus on being present and open to the experience, allowing it to rejuvenate your spirit.

- **<u>Scripture Study</u>**: Dive deeper into the Bible by joining a study group or setting personal reading goals. Approach the scripture with curiosity and an open heart, seeking to understand and apply its teachings in your daily life.

- **<u>Community Involvement</u>**: Reconnect with your faith community through shared activities and experiences. Participate in group discussions, volunteer for service projects, and support each other in your spiritual journeys.

- **<u>Acts of Service</u>**: Engage in service to others as a tangible expression of your faith. Whether it's volunteering at a local charity or simply helping a neighbor, these acts of kindness reinforce your sense of purpose and connection to the world.

- **<u>Personal Reflection</u>**: Regularly take time to reflect on your spiritual journey. Consider keeping a journal where you can explore your thoughts, experiences, and growth over time. This practice helps to clarify your goals and keeps you aligned with your spiritual values.

By integrating these practices into your life, you can stoke the flames of your spiritual passion and cultivate a deeper, more meaningful connection with your faith. Remember, this journey is personal and unique to you, and each step you take brings you closer to a more vibrant and fulfilling spiritual existence.

- **Remember Your Testimony:** as we revisit the powerful moments of our testimonies, let us reflect on our first encounters with Christ, recalling the immense joy, profound peace, and the incredible sense of purpose that filled our hearts then and continue to resonate within us. By sharing these powerful accounts and experiences within the heart of our community, we can reignite the collective passion and shared purpose that binds us together.

Through these stories, we weave a rich tapestry of faith, each thread representing personal triumphs and challenges overcome in the light of divine guidance. Let us take this opportunity to listen actively, offering support and encouragement to one another as we navigate our spiritual journeys. In doing so, we not only strengthen our individual connections to God but also fortify the bonds that unite us as a faith community.

These testimonies serve as reminders of the transformational power inherent in our faith, highlighting both the struggles we have faced and the grace that has carried us through. They are living proof that, regardless of where we find ourselves on our spiritual path, there is always hope for renewal and growth.

As we gather to share our stories, we create a space for vulnerability and authenticity, where each voice is valued and every experience is honored. This openness fosters an environment of trust and mutual respect, essential ingredients for a thriving and dynamic faith community. Together, we can build a foundation of shared understanding and empathy, where the lessons learned from one person's journey can illuminate the way for others.

Let us celebrate these moments of connection, recognizing that they are not merely reflections of the past but seeds of inspiration for the future. By embracing our collective narratives, we empower each other to continue seeking deeper, more meaningful engagement with our faith. In this way, our community becomes a beacon of love and hope, shining brightly in a world in need of compassion and light.

May our testimonies inspire us to live out our faith with renewed vigor and commitment, motivating us to act as instruments of peace and vessels of God's boundless love. Let us go forward, emboldened by the stories we've shared, ready to face the challenges ahead with a spirit of joy and resilience, confident in the knowledge that we walk this path together, united in purpose and faith.

- **Intentional Worship:** is more than simply going through the motions; it's about engaging in a heartfelt, loving response to God's grace and mercy. This might involve investigating various forms of worship, such as musical expression, artistic creation, or shared communal experiences, to find those that best connect with and reflect our current spiritual condition.

A Personal Anecdote:

"During a children's service, a little girl tugged my sleeve and asked, 'Why doesn't anybody dance when we sing about Jesus?' I paused, stunned by her insight. She wasn't being cute—she was being honest. In her world, joy and movement were natural expressions of love. That one question burned into my soul: What had we lost when worship became stillness?"

By exploring these diverse avenues, we open ourselves up to new ways of experiencing and expressing our faith, allowing us to connect with the divine in a manner that resonates deeply with our souls.

- **<u>Musical expression</u>**, for instance, can be a powerful form of worship. Whether through singing hymns, playing instruments, or simply listening to spiritually uplifting music, these melodies and harmonies can elevate our spirits and draw us closer to God. Music has the unique ability to transcend words, touching our hearts and stirring emotions that words alone may fail to capture.

- **<u>Artistic creation</u>**, likewise, provides a profound channel for worship. Through painting, drawing, sculpture, or any other form of artistic endeavor, we can express our devotion and gratitude to God. This creative process allows us to reflect on our spiritual journey, using our talents to honor the Creator and to communicate aspects of our faith that might be difficult to articulate otherwise.

- **<u>Shared communal experiences,</u>** such as group worship services, retreats, or community celebrations, offer opportunities to worship collectively. In these settings, we find strength in numbers, drawing inspiration from the shared energy and enthusiasm of our fellow believers. These gatherings remind us of the importance of community and the joy of worshipping together, reinforcing our sense of belonging and purpose within the faith collective.

Ultimately, intentional worship is about seeking a genuine connection with God, one that is sincere and meaningful. It invites us to be present, to open our hearts fully, and to engage with our faith in a way that is both personal and profound. As we explore different forms of worship, let us do so with an open heart and a curious spirit, embracing the journey of discovery and enrichment that lies ahead.

- **<u>Deepening one's scriptural engagement</u>** by consistently studying the Bible—whether through the structure of small groups or the personal practice of devotionals—invites a more profound understanding and fosters a stronger connection with the promises and commands found within God's word.

- **<u>By actively participating in outreach programs and service projects</u>**, we can rediscover our sense of purpose and strengthen our bonds within the community, thus serving others and ourselves. As we dedicate our efforts towards improving the lives of others, we simultaneously cultivate a richer and more profound personal experience of our faith.

This act of giving and serving not only benefits those we help but also enriches our own spiritual journey, allowing us to see God's work in action and experience the joy of selflessness. By stepping outside of our comfort zones and extending a helping hand, we open ourselves to new perspectives and deepen our empathy and compassion.

Furthermore, engaging in these activities encourages us to reflect on the core teachings of our faith, prompting us to live out the Gospel's call to love our neighbors as ourselves. As we witness the transformative impact of our collective efforts, we become more aware of the interconnectedness of our community and the vital role each of us plays in fostering a supportive and nurturing environment.

Let this commitment to service be a reminder of the abundant grace we have received and the opportunity we have to share that grace with others. Through each act of kindness and generosity, we not only uplift those in need but also reinforce our own spiritual resilience and dedication.

As we continue to explore these avenues of engagement, may we do so with humility and a sincere desire to embody the teachings of Christ. Let our actions reflect the light of His love, serving as beacons of hope and inspiration to all we encounter. Together, let us create a legacy of faith-filled service that resonates throughout our community and beyond, leaving a lasting impact for generations to come.

- **<u>To create accountability within our faith</u>**, it's essential to cultivate strong relationships with fellow believers who will both inspire and challenge us as we journey together in our commitment to Christ. Honest fellowship, a place where we can openly share our doubts and struggles, is incredibly beneficial in renewing and reinvigorating our commitment.

These connections provide a safe haven where vulnerability is met with understanding and compassion, allowing us to grow and learn from each other's experiences. In this nurturing environment, we find the courage to confront our spiritual apathy and the motivation to reignite our passion for our faith.

Moreover, such relationships often serve as mirrors, reflecting the areas in our lives that require attention and growth. Our fellow believers can lovingly hold us accountable, encouraging us to stay true to our spiritual disciplines and reminding us of the commitments we have made. This mutual support fosters an atmosphere of growth, where we are both supported and stretched in our spiritual journeys.

- **<u>To foster these meaningful connections</u>**, we must be intentional in our interactions, seeking out opportunities for deep, authentic conversation. Whether through small groups, prayer meetings, or informal gatherings, these moments of connection can become catalysts for spiritual renewal. As we share our triumphs and trials, we build a network of support that empowers us to face challenges with resilience and hope.

Ultimately, by surrounding ourselves with a community of believers who genuinely care for our well-being, we create a foundation of accountability that not only strengthens our individual faith but also enriches the collective spirit of our community. Together, we can journey forward with confidence, knowing that we are not alone and that our shared commitment to Christ binds us together in love and purpose.

In this chapter, we will explore the insidious roots of apathy, those subtle tendencies that slowly suffocate our spiritual lives, while simultaneously illuminating the vibrant pathways that lead us back to a spirited and fervent faith, a journey of rediscovery and renewal.

In the following sections, we will delve into a comprehensive examination of how busyness, constant distractions, and a pervasive sense of spiritual fatigue can collectively contribute to the development of emotional and spiritual detachment. Like a fire needing fuel, our relationship with Christ needs dedicated effort and consistent community involvement.

Through these explorations, we aim to identify the underlying causes that often go unnoticed yet significantly impact our spiritual vitality. We will consider how modern life's demands can overshadow our spiritual priorities, leading us to a state of complacency where once vibrant faith becomes a mere routine.

The hustle and bustle of daily life can easily eclipse our spiritual pursuits, often leaving us feeling disconnected from our faith community and, ultimately, from God Himself. This disconnection can manifest as a gradual erosion of our spiritual disciplines—prayer becomes sporadic, scripture study is sidelined, and communal worship is seen as optional rather than essential. Recognizing these patterns is the first step in combating apathy and reclaiming the dynamic relationship with Christ that we are called to nurture.

In our journey to counteract this drift, we must rediscover the joy and fulfillment that come from living a faith-centered life. By intentionally creating space for spiritual practices, we replenish our spiritual reserves and rekindle our passion for God. This involves not only personal reflection and devotion but also engaging actively with our community, drawing strength from collective worship and shared experiences.

Moreover, we will explore how embracing a rhythm of rest and renewal can combat the fatigue that often accompanies spiritual apathy. By honoring the Sabbath and integrating moments of rest into our daily lives, we create opportunities to recharge and to refocus our hearts and minds on what truly matters.

Our exploration will also highlight the role of gratitude in sustaining a vibrant faith. By cultivating a thankful heart, we shift our perspective from scarcity to abundance, recognizing the countless blessings in our lives and the grace that sustains us through every trial.

As we delve into these themes, let us remain open to the transformative possibilities that lie ahead. Together, we will chart a course towards a revitalized faith, one that not only withstands the pressures of modern life but thrives in the midst of them. Through intentional action and community support, we can reignite the flame of our spiritual passion, illuminating our paths with the light of Christ's love and purpose.

In this session, we will delve into the significance of prayer, consistent scripture study, and meaningful fellowship, exploring how these practices contribute to fostering a profoundly personal and enriching relationship with God.

As we come together, let us acknowledge the serious threat of apathy, recognizing how it harms our personal development, hindering our capacity to help others, and let us recommit ourselves to rekindling our passion for the Gospel, understanding that our spiritual energy is not merely for our own benefit—providing personal solace and confidence—but is also essential for the world, which urgently needs the guiding light of Christ.

In this session, we will delve into practical strategies designed to foster a deeper, more passionate, and engaged relationship with our faith, enhancing our ability to serve as effective witnesses, and radiating God's love and grace to others.

Through this exploration, we invite you to embark on a transformative journey—one that not only addresses the roots of apathy but also empowers you to cultivate a vibrant and fulfilling spiritual life. By intentionally choosing to nurture our faith, we can create ripples of positive change that extend far beyond ourselves, impacting our communities and the wider world.

Together, we will examine the foundational practices that can reignite our spiritual fervor and equip us to meet the challenges of apathy with resilience and hope.

- We begin with **the power of prayer**—a direct line to God that nourishes our spirit and grounds us in His presence. Prayer is not just a ritual; it is a heartfelt dialogue that invites us to share our deepest thoughts and desires with our Creator. As we pray, we open ourselves to divine wisdom, finding guidance and peace that transcend our earthly concerns.

- **Consistent scripture study** is another cornerstone of a vibrant faith. By immersing ourselves in the Word of God, we gain a clearer understanding of His promises and commands, drawing strength and inspiration from the stories of faith that have shaped generations. This practice encourages us to apply biblical teachings in our daily lives, fostering a closer alignment with God's will and a deeper appreciation of His unending love.

- **<u>Meaningful fellowship</u>**, meanwhile, provides the communal support that is vital for spiritual growth. Engaging with others who share our faith journey helps to hold us accountable and to inspire us with fresh perspectives. Whether through small groups, church gatherings, or informal discussions, these connections offer a space for encouragement, challenge, and mutual edification.

As we delve into these practices, let us recognize that our spiritual vitality is not just a personal endeavor; it is a collective journey. Our renewed passion and commitment to the Gospel can illuminate the lives of those around us, offering hope and love in a world often marked by darkness and despair. By actively participating in our faith communities and serving others, we become conduits of God's grace, bringing His light into the world.

Our exploration is an invitation to embrace transformation, to shake off the shackles of apathy, and to step boldly into a life filled with purpose and joy. Let us commit to nurturing our relationship with God, understanding that each step we take towards Him brings us closer to a life that is not only personally fulfilling but also richly impactful to those we encounter. As we journey together, may we be inspired to live out our faith with authenticity and passion, reflecting the transformative power of the Gospel in all that we do.

As we progress, remember that every step taken towards rekindling our spiritual fervor is a step towards living out our true purpose with renewed zeal and commitment. Let us embrace this opportunity for growth, knowing that each small effort contributes to a larger tapestry of faith, woven together by acts of love, service, and devotion. Together, we can overcome the challenges of apathy and reignite our passion for a life that reflects the transformative power of the Gospel.

With this understanding, let's consider how we can practically implement these insights into our daily lives, creating a rhythm that consistently nurtures our spiritual well-being. Begin by setting aside a few moments each day to pause and reflect, allowing yourself to reconnect with the source of your faith. This could be as simple as starting your morning with a quiet meditation on scripture or ending your day with a prayer of gratitude.

- Additionally, **seek out opportunities for intentional connection with your faith community**. Whether it's participating in a small group study, attending a worship service, or volunteering together, these interactions can provide the encouragement and accountability needed to sustain your spiritual journey. Engaging with others who share your faith not only strengthens your own resolve but also fuels a collective passion that can drive meaningful change within your community.

- Furthermore, **consider incorporating acts of service into your routine**. Whether big or small, these actions serve as outward expressions of your inward faith, demonstrating the love and compassion that are central to the Gospel. As you serve others, you may find that your own spirit is lifted, revealing new depths of empathy and understanding.

- **Lastly, be mindful of the need for rest and renewal.** In a world that often glorifies busyness, make it a priority to honor moments of stillness and reflection. Embrace the Sabbath as a time to recharge, not just physically, but

spiritually, allowing yourself to be refreshed and reinvig-
orated for the work ahead.

By weaving these practices into the fabric of your daily life, you
create a sustainable rhythm that not only counters spiritual apathy but also cultivates a vibrant, thriving faith. Let us move
forward, confident in the knowledge that our journey is not
taken alone, but with a community that supports and uplifts us.
Together, we can shine brightly, illuminating the world with the
hope and love of Christ.

Our journey is one of hope and renewal, a reminder that even
in the face of spiritual lethargy, we can rediscover the joy and
energy that first drew us to our faith. May this chapter serve
as a beacon of encouragement, guiding you towards a deeper
connection with God and a more profound experience of His
love, grace, and purpose for your life.

As we conclude this exploration of spiritual apathy and its antidotes, let us look forward with optimism and determination.
Remember, the path to rekindling your spiritual fire is

not a solitary one. It is walked hand in hand with your community, supported by the shared stories of faith, challenges, and triumphs. Engage actively in your spiritual practices, knowing that each prayer, act of service, and moment of reflection is a step towards a more vibrant and fulfilling spiritual existence.

Consider each day an opportunity to renew your commitment, to choose love and understanding over indifference and isolation. Let the light of your reawakened passion illuminate the paths of others, inspiring them to embark on their own journeys of faith and discovery. Together, let us foster an environment where spiritual growth is celebrated, and where the strength of our community becomes a testament to the enduring power of faith.

As you move forward, carry with you the wisdom gleaned from this chapter, and let it inform your actions and decisions. Trust that every effort you make to deepen your spiritual engagement will not only transform your own life but also ripple outwards, touching the lives of those around you. In doing so, you become a living expression of the Gospel, a beacon of hope and a testament to the transformative power of unwavering faith.

Chapter Three

Two-Alarm Fire

The Spread of Division

As the echoes of the first alarm fade, a second alarm ignites—a piercing call to attention, signaling the growing divisions within the Church. This alarm serves as a stark reminder that discord and conflict, much like a wildfire, can spread quickly through the weak points in our fellowship, consuming the unity that Christ so fervently prayed for. In John 17:21, Jesus implores the Father, "that they may all be one, just as you, Father, are in me, and I in you, that they also may be in us, so that the world may believe that you have sent me." This profound plea underscores the importance of unity, not merely as an ideal, but as an essential foundation for our collective witness to the world.

Together, we must confront this challenge head-on, recognizing that our unity is not just for our own benefit, but for the sake of our witness to the world. As we strive to embody the unity Jesus prayed for, let us remember that each member of our community plays a vital role in this endeavor. Our differences need not be divisive; instead, they can be a source of strength when approached with love and respect.

In this chapter, we will delve deeper into the dynamics of division and explore how we can transform potential pitfalls into opportunities for growth. Through understanding and addressing the root causes of discord, we can begin to dismantle the barriers that threaten our unity.

By embracing a spirit of reconciliation and commitment to each other, we can overcome the challenges that lie ahead. Let us encourage one another, hold fast to the teachings of Christ, and work tirelessly to ensure that our Church remains a beacon of hope and love in a world that desperately needs it. We are called to be peacemakers, bridge-builders, and stewards of the grace that has been so generously given to us.

The fabric of our Church is woven together by the threads of relationships—each one important, each one vulnerable. When misunderstandings arise, or when personal grievances are allowed to fester, the potential for division increases. This chapter will examine common sources of conflict within the Church, offering insight into their nature and urgency. As we move deeper into this examination, we must remember that reconciliation is not just an option; it is a mandate that our faith compels us to pursue.

One of the most common sources of conflict within the Church stems from differences in interpretation and application of Scripture. These differences, often rooted in personal convictions and cultural backgrounds, can lead to passionate debates. While vigorous discussion can enrich our faith, it can also sow seeds of division if not approached with a spirit of humility and love.

A Personal Anecdote:

"There was a time I stood behind the pulpit with a sermon fully written, cross-referenced, and polished. But as I looked out, I sensed a weight in the room—not from the congregation, but from with-

in. The words I had prepared felt hollow. That day, I preached truth—but without fire. And I knew it. It was a humbling awakening: conviction must first be ignited in the messenger before it can kindle anyone else."

Another source of discord is the struggle for power and influence. Leadership roles within the Church are meant to be positions of service, yet human nature can sometimes transform them into arenas for personal ambition. This can result in factions forming, each vying for control and recognition, rather than focusing on the shared mission of serving God and His people.

Personal grievances, if left unaddressed, can also become a breeding ground for division. Minor offenses or misunderstandings, when not reconciled, can grow into major rifts that disrupt the harmony of our community. It's crucial to address these issues promptly and with compassion, seeking to understand and forgive.

As we explore these sources of conflict, let us be reminded that our response to them is what truly matters. We are called to create a culture where reconciliation is the norm. By actively pursuing healing and understanding, we can transform potential divisions into opportunities for deeper connection and unity.

In the pages ahead, we will examine these dynamics in greater detail, providing practical steps and biblical guidance to navigate the challenges of division. Our goal is to equip the Church with the tools necessary to foster an environment where love prevails over discord, and unity triumphs over separation. Let us journey together, with open hearts and minds, towards a more unified and strengthened community of faith.

Understanding Division

Division often creeps in unnoticed, often masked by our busyness and familiarity with one another. Disagreements over doctrine, practices, or leadership styles can begin as minor disagreements but can escalate into significant rifts if left unaddressed. It's imperative to remember that the Church is comprised of individuals with diverse backgrounds and experiences, all joining together under the banner of Christ. This diversity, while beautiful, can sometimes lead to misunderstandings.

Take, for example, the different interpretations of Scripture that arise among sincere believers. While this diversity can enrich our understanding, it can also lead to contention when we fail to approach each other with grace. Paul reminds us in Ephesians 4:3 to be eager to maintain the unity of the Spirit in the bond of peace. It is this peace that must permeate our interactions, but oftentimes, pride and self-interest get in the way.

When pride overshadows humility, the seeds of division find fertile ground. It's crucial, then, to cultivate a spirit of humility and openness, where we place the collective well-being of the Church above our individual preferences. This does not mean abandoning our convictions but rather engaging in dialogue that seeks to understand and appreciate different perspectives.

Consider the example of early Church councils, where leaders from diverse backgrounds gathered to discuss and resolve theological disputes. These gatherings were not without tension, yet they were underpinned by a shared commitment to unity and truth. Their efforts remind us that, while disagreements are inevitable, they need not lead to division if approached with a spirit of collaboration and mutual respect.

In our own communities today, we must strive to emulate this example by fostering environments where differences are not merely tolerated but celebrated as opportunities for mutual growth and learning. By doing so, we can transform potential conflicts into avenues for deeper fellowship and shared purpose.

It is love that binds us together, as evidenced by the many "one another" passages in the New Testament, encouraging us to bear with, forgive, and spur one another on toward love and good deeds. As we navigate the complexities of modern Church life, let us commit to embodying these principles, ensuring that our diversity becomes a testament to the beauty of God's creation rather than a source of division.

Strategies for Reconciliation

Fostering reconciliation is a proactive approach to countering division. Here are several strategies that can aid in restoring relationships among believers:

1. Cultivate a Culture of Open Communication: Encourage an environment where individuals feel safe expressing their thoughts and feelings. Create platforms for dialogue—whether through small groups or church meetings—where honest discussions can take place without fear of retribution.

2. Practice Active Listening: Listening is more than hearing words; it involves understanding the emotion and intention behind them. Encourage congregants to engage in active listening. This means acknowledging others' perspectives, even when disagreements arise.

3. Seek Common Ground: In conflicts, it can be easy to focus on differences. Instead, redirect the conversation toward common beliefs and values that unite rather than divide. Highlighting shared convictions fosters connection and diminishes animosity.

4. Embrace Humility and Accountability: Encourage individuals to approach conflicts with humility. Recognizing one's own faults and being accountable for one's actions can break down barriers of pride and lead to healing.

5. Model Forgiveness: Christ exemplified forgiveness. Encourage forgiveness as a central tenet of your community. Remind one another that we are all imperfect, and just as we have received grace, we must extend it to others.

6. Promote Empathy and Understanding: Strive to see situations from others' perspectives. Encouraging empathy helps to build bridges of understanding and compassion, allowing us to respond with kindness and consideration. When we walk in each other's shoes, we are more likely to find paths toward reconciliation.

A Personal Anecdote:

"While visiting a congregant's home, I noticed a Bible sitting beneath a stack of old newspapers and unopened mail. Gently, I

picked it up. The pages still bore markings from a faithful season long past. I asked the gentleman, 'When was the last time this book spoke to you?' He replied quietly, 'It hasn't in years... but maybe I stopped listening.' That moment reminded me: conviction doesn't disappear overnight—it dims through neglect."

7. Facilitate Mediation and Conflict Resolution: Sometimes, conflicts benefit from the involvement of a neutral third party. Consider appointing trusted leaders or trained mediators who can guide discussions and help navigate complex issues with wisdom and impartiality.

8. Celebrate Diversity: Acknowledge and celebrate the diversity within your community. Host events or activities that highlight diverse cultures, traditions, and viewpoints. By appreciating the richness that diversity brings, you can foster a sense of belonging and unity.

9. Encourage Prayer and Spiritual Reflection: Encourage members to seek guidance through prayer and spiritual reflection. Prayer can soften hearts and open minds, providing divine insight and peace in times of discord. A community that prays together stays connected to its spiritual foundation.

10. Build Strong Relationships: Invest time in building genuine relationships within your community. Strong bonds create a supportive network that can weather disagreements and challenges. Encourage fellowship opportunities, such as retreats or social gatherings, to strengthen these connections.

A Personal Anecdote:

"A college student approached me after service and said, 'I love coming here... but do you ever feel like you're holding back?' His honesty startled me—not because it was disrespectful, but because it was right. In his hunger for real truth, I heard the cry of a generation. That encounter convicted me deeply: the gospel deserves boldness, not dilution."

By implementing these strategies, we can create a Church environment where reconciliation is prioritized, and unity is cherished. As we commit to these practices, let us be reminded of the words of Colossians 3:14: "And over all these virtues put on love, which binds them all together in perfect unity." With love as our guiding principle, we can navigate the complexities of our differences and emerge as a stronger, more unified body of believers.

In embracing this journey toward unity, we must also be patient with ourselves and others. True reconciliation takes time and effort, requiring us to be steadfast in our commitment to nurturing relationships. Let us remember that every small step toward understanding and peace is significant and adds to the collective strength of our community.

To truly embody the unity that Christ envisioned, we must also engage in continual self-reflection and growth. It is essential to examine our own hearts and attitudes, ensuring that we are contributing positively to the fabric of our Church. By doing so, we create an environment where love and respect are the norm, and where every individual feels valued and heard.

As we move forward, let us be vigilant in fostering a culture that celebrates diversity and encourages meaningful connections. In doing so, we not only honor the teachings of Christ but also build a Church that serves as a beacon of hope and love to the world around us. Together, with hearts united by love, we can overcome any challenge and shine brightly as a testament to the transformative power of faith and unity.

Conclusion: The Call to Unity

As the second alarm sounds, let it not be a call to despair, but a clarion call to action. The health of our Church depends on our commitment to unity and reconciliation. Embracing the teachings of Jesus about oneness should inspire us to work diligently to mend broken relationships, foster understanding, and create an atmosphere where love can flourish.

In the chapters that follow, we will explore practical applications and testimonies of reconciliation in action, reminding us that while divisions may threaten to spread like a wildfire, the power of Christ's love can extinguish conflict and restore harmony within His body. Our collective mission is not just to survive the flames of division but to emerge from them transformed—more united and resilient than before.

We are called to be active participants in this transformative journey, embracing the challenge with faith and determination. As we delve into these stories of reconciliation, let us draw inspiration from those who have walked the path before us, learning from their experiences and triumphs.

In our quest for unity, we must be vigilant, recognizing the subtle signs of division and addressing them with urgency and grace. We are tasked with the responsibility of being both guardians and nurturers of the bonds that tie us together. Through prayer, dialogue, and mutual support, we can create a community where differences are appreciated, and conflicts are resolved with compassion.

As we turn the pages of this journey, let us do so with hearts open to change, minds ready to learn, and spirits eager to embrace the unity that Christ envisioned. Together, we can build a Church that not only withstands the trials of discord but shines brightly as a testament to the love and grace that binds us all.

In the chapters ahead, we will witness how individuals and congregations have navigated the turbulent waters of division with
courage and grace. Their stories will serve as both a testament to
the power of reconciliation and a guide for our own efforts to
foster unity.

We'll examine case studies where churches have successfully ad-
dressed conflicts, highlighting the strategies and attitudes that
led to healing and renewed fellowship. These accounts will offer
practical insights and encouragement, demonstrating that reconciliation is not only possible but profoundly transformative.

As we explore these narratives, let us remain mindful of the vital
role that love plays in our journey. It is love that compels us
to reach across divides, to listen with empathy, and to act with
compassion. Love is the thread that weaves us together into a
tapestry of diverse yet unified believers.

Throughout this exploration, we will also revisit the biblical
teachings that underscore our call to unity. Scriptures will serve
as our compass, reminding us of the foundational principles that

guide our interactions with one another. By grounding our efforts in these teachings, we can ensure that our path toward reconciliation is both faithful and fruitful.

Let us carry forward the hope that, through our collective efforts, we can create a Church that truly reflects the heart of Christ—a community that is welcoming, inclusive, and unwavering in its commitment to love and unity. As we embark on this journey, may we be inspired to not only seek reconciliation within our own communities but also to extend this spirit of unity to the world beyond our doors.

Together, as we continue to learn, grow, and strive for harmony, we can become a living testament to the transformative power of faith, unity, and love.

SONNET FOR A TWO-ALARM FIRE

Charles E. Cravey

Where flames dance fiercely in the night's embrace,
A mighty foe that roars with untamed might.

Its crimson tendrils reach with fiery grace,
Turning the darkened sky a vivid light.

Brave souls arise, with courage in their eyes,
To battle heat and smoke with every breath,
Against the blaze that leaps toward the skies,
Defying all the threats of fiery death.

Their sirens wail, a clarion call of hope,
As water streams to quench the blazing ire.
Together, side by side, they learn to cope,
And face the fearsome wrath of two-alarm fire.

In unity, they stand and fight the storm,
Until the night is safe, and hearts are warm.

Chapter Four

Three-Alarm Fire

The Threat of Worldliness

SONNET FOR A THREE-ALARM FIRE

Charles E. Cravey

Where flames dance wildly in the midnight air,
Their fiery tongues consume with fierce desire.
A crackling symphony that none can bear,
Yet still we watch, entranced by nature's pyre.

The sirens wail, a call to arms so brave,
As heroes rush to tame the blazing beast,

Their courage shines, a testament to save,
The lives and dreams that might be soon deceased.

The smoke ascends, a cloud of dark despair,
Yet through the haze, a sense of hope remains.
For even in destruction's harshest glare,
The human spirit triumphs over pain.

From ashes rise the seeds of strength anew,
A testament to all that we can do.

In today's fast-paced world, the threat of worldliness can feel like a smoldering ember, waiting for the right moment to ignite and consume our spiritual integrity. The allure of secular values is pervasive, slipping into our hearts and minds through subtle channels such as media, popular culture, and even the norms of our communities. Just as a fire gains strength from combustible materials, so too can the values of the world weaken our witness for Christ, extinguishing the light we are called to share.

A Personal Anecdote:

"Years ago, I witnessed a church vote that split a congregation in

half. It wasn't about doctrine or moral failing—it was about personality and pride. Good people left, friendships unraveled, and the sanctuary felt colder for months. I remember standing in the pulpit and sensing not just grief, but guilt. Division doesn't need heresy to flourish—it only needs hearts unwilling to yield."

To combat this, we must remain vigilant, nurturing the flame of our faith with intentional practices that resist conformity to worldly patterns. This involves consistently seeking wisdom through prayer and the study of Scripture, allowing these disciplines to fuel our spiritual resilience. Moreover, cultivating meaningful relationships with fellow believers serves as a buffer against the isolating effects of a culture that often prizes individualism over community. By fostering environments where faith is openly shared and celebrated, we create a network of support that strengthens our collective resolve.

The challenge lies not in withdrawing from the world but in engaging with it from a place of spiritual strength and clarity. By doing so, we can transform potential threats into opportunities for growth, allowing our lives to be a testament to the enduring truth and love of Christ. As we navigate the complexities of modern life, let us remain steadfast in our commitment to live authentically and faithfully, ever mindful of the impact our choices have on our spiritual journey and the world around us.

At the heart of this discussion is the biblical imperative found in **John 15:19**, where Jesus warns His disciples, ***"If you were of the world, the world would love you as its own; but because you are not of the world, but I chose you out of the world, therefore the world hates you."*** This verse underscores our dual role as followers of Christ—we are to inhabit the world, engaging with it, yet our lives should reflect our distinct identity as children of God.

A Personal Anecdote:

"I'll never forget a youth-led service where an elderly woman stood and sang 'Great Is Thy Faithfulness.' The band followed her lead, and soon teens and elders were singing together—tears flowing freely. That moment reminded me: unity isn't always forged in meetings—it's born in shared worship, when hearts forget their age and sing in one Spirit."

Understanding Worldliness

Worldliness does not merely refer to a specific set of actions or be-haviors; it encompasses a mindset deeply rooted in the values and priorities of a society that often stands in contrast to the teachings of Christ. It can manifest in various forms—materialism, moral relativism, and the pursuit of personal success at the expense of community and spiritual health. Recognizing these influences is the first step toward guarding our hearts and minds.

To effectively counteract worldliness, it is essential to cultivate an awareness of its subtle encroachments in our daily lives. This means being intentional about the choices we make and the val-ues we uphold. By prioritizing spiritual growth and aligning our lives with the teachings of Christ, we can develop a resilient faith that withstands external pressures.

A crucial aspect of this journey is fostering a mindset that values eternal truths over temporary gains. This involves a conscious effort to evaluate our motivations and desires, ensuring they align with our faith rather than fleeting societal trends. By doing so, we can focus on nurturing virtues such as humility, gratitude, and compassion, which serve as antidotes to the self-centered tendencies promoted by worldly influences.

Furthermore, engaging in regular self-reflection and prayer allows us to remain grounded in our identity as Christians. It offers us the opportunity to recalibrate our hearts and minds, seeking guidance and strength from God to resist the allure of worldliness. In this way, we can live out our faith authentically, becoming beacons of hope and light in a world that often prioritizes darkness over truth.

By embracing our calling to live counter-culturally, we not only protect our spiritual well-being but also inspire others to seek the transformative power of a life rooted in Christ. Together, let us endeavor to create communities that reflect His love and truth, serving as a testament to the enduring impact of a life devoted to God.

The Call to Be Distinct

Our distinctiveness as believers is not about isolating ourselves from society but about being countercultural in our practices and values. We are called to reflect the character of Christ in a world that frequently opts for convenience over conviction. This means demonstrating love, grace, and truth in our interactions while remaining steadfast in our core beliefs.

By doing so, we become living examples of the transformative power of faith, illustrating how a life grounded in Christ can inspire positive change around us. Our actions and decisions should be guided by principles that transcend popular trends, offering a beacon of stability and hope to those searching for meaning.

In practical terms, this distinctiveness is expressed through acts of kindness and compassion, choosing to forgive rather than hold grudges, and seeking justice in a manner that uplifts rather than divides. It means engaging in conversations with empathy, listening to understand rather than to respond, and standing firm in our beliefs without resorting to hostility or judgment.

As we navigate our daily lives, we must be mindful of the influence we have on others. Our conduct can either draw people closer to the love of Christ or push them away. Therefore, let us strive to embody the values of the kingdom of God, always seeking to build bridges and foster understanding.

Our goal is to create a ripple effect of goodness and faithfulness that extends beyond our immediate circles, touching the lives of those we encounter. By living authentically and courageously in accordance with our faith, we not only honor God but also offer a compelling testimony of His enduring love and grace to a watching world.

One powerful way to maintain our identity is by immersing ourselves in biblical teachings and fostering genuine community bonds within our congregations. In doing so, we create a supportive environment where accountability and encouragement flow freely, empowering members to resist the pull of worldly influences.

By building such a nurturing community, we not only strengthen our own faith but also create a welcoming space for others to explore and grow in their relationship with Christ. This sense of belonging is crucial, as it provides a foundation for individuals to develop a deeper understanding of their faith and its application in everyday life.

Moreover, these community bonds serve as a reminder of our shared mission to embody the love and teachings of Jesus. When we gather in fellowship, we are reminded of the importance of lifting each other up, celebrating victories, and supporting one another through challenges. This mutual support is vital in a world that often encourages isolation and self-reliance.

In fostering such an environment, we also open the door to diverse perspectives and experiences that enrich our collective journey. By embracing differences and learning from each other, we strengthen the fabric of our community and reflect the inclusive nature of the gospel. As we continue to grow together, our unity becomes a powerful testament to the transformative power of living out our faith in a world yearning for genuine connection and hope.

As we lean into these biblical teachings and cultivate authentic relationships, we equip ourselves and others to stand firm in our faith, radiating the light and truth of Christ in every area of our lives.

Strategies to Resist Worldliness

1. Engagement with Scripture: Regularly reading and meditating on the Bible equips us with the knowledge to discern truth from falsehood. The more we understand God's Word, the better prepared we are to stand against societal pressures.

Engaging with Scripture is not just about acquiring knowledge; it's about allowing the Word of God to transform our hearts and minds. When we delve into the Bible with an open heart, we invite the Holy Spirit to guide us in understanding and applying its truths in our lives. This spiritual discipline fosters wisdom and discernment, empowering us to navigate the complexities of modern life with grace and conviction.

By embedding Scripture into our daily routines, we build a solid foundation of faith that withstands the shifting sands of cultural norms. As we reflect on biblical teachings, we gain insights that challenge our perspectives and inspire us to live in alignment with God's will. This ongoing engagement with God's Word becomes a source of strength, enabling us to resist the allure of worldliness and stay true to our calling.

Moreover, studying Scripture in community with others can enhance our spiritual journey. Sharing insights, asking questions, and discussing interpretations with fellow believers create a rich tapestry of learning and growth. This collaborative approach not only deepens our understanding but also fosters a sense of unity and shared purpose as we seek to embody the teachings of Christ.

By prioritizing our engagement with Scripture, we equip ourselves to be effective ambassadors of faith, capable of influencing the world around us with love, truth, and integrity. Let us embrace this vital practice, allowing the Word of God to illuminate our paths and guide us towards a life that reflects the heart of Christ.

2. Intentional Community: Surrounding ourselves with fellow believers who share our commitment to Christ can provide the necessary support to resist worldly temptations. Fellowship, prayer, and shared experiences strengthen our resolve.

When we engage in intentional community, we create a space where our faith can flourish amidst the challenges of the world. These communities become sanctuaries of encouragement, where we find accountability partners who lovingly guide us back on track when we falter. By sharing our lives with others who are dedicated to walking the path of faith, we draw strength from one another, finding inspiration in each other's stories and experiences.

This fellowship goes beyond mere social gatherings; it is about forming deep, meaningful relationships that are rooted in love and mutual support. Through regular prayer meetings, Bible studies, and shared service projects, we cultivate a sense of belonging and purpose. These interactions remind us that we are not alone in our journey and that our struggles are shared by those who walk alongside us.

Moreover, intentional community is a powerful witness to the world. As we live out our faith together, we demonstrate the beauty and strength of collective spiritual life. Our unity and love for one another serve as a compelling testament to the transformative power of Christ's teachings.

In times of doubt or difficulty, these communities provide a refuge where we can find solace and guidance. They challenge us to grow, to become more like Christ, and to extend His love to those beyond our immediate circles. By investing in these relationships, we not only fortify our own faith but also create a ripple effect that inspires others to seek the same depth of connection and purpose.

Intentional community is not just about personal growth; it is about building the kingdom of God here on earth. Together, we can shine as a light in the darkness, offering hope, compassion, and truth to a world in need.

3. Critical Media Consumption: Being mindful of the media we consume—movies, music, books—can help mitigate the influence of secular values. Choosing content that aligns with our

Christian values nurtures our spiritual growth and reinforces our identity.

In a world saturated with diverse media offerings, it's imperative for us to approach our consumption with discernment and intentionality. By actively selecting content that uplifts and aligns with our faith, we not only protect our hearts and minds but also cultivate an environment that fosters spiritual growth. This doesn't mean avoiding all secular media but engaging with it critically and thoughtfully.

When we evaluate the media we engage with, we should consider its underlying messages and the values it promotes. Does it encourage virtues such as love, kindness, and integrity, or does it glorify themes that could undermine our faith? By being selective, we can fill our minds with content that inspires and challenges us to live out our beliefs more fully.

Moreover, discussing media with fellow believers can be an enriching experience. It offers the opportunity to share perspectives, deepen understanding, and explore how different stories and narratives can illuminate aspects of our faith. This collaborative approach not only enhances our media literacy but also strengthens our community bonds, as we navigate these cultural waters together.

By practicing critical media consumption, we empower ourselves to remain steadfast in our commitment to Christ, even amidst a media landscape that often contradicts our values. Let us strive to be mindful of what we allow into our hearts and minds, ensuring that our choices reflect our dedication to living a life that honors God.

4. Service and Outreach: Actively living out our faith in service to others helps to solidify our place in the world while keeping our focus on Christ. Engaging in outreach programs for our communities highlights love and compassion, attributes that resonate with the heart of the gospel.

When we participate in acts of service and outreach, we embody the teachings of Jesus, who called us to serve "the least of these." This commitment to helping others not only strengthens our faith but also serves as a practical expression of Christ's love in action. By stepping outside of our comfort zones to meet the needs of those around us, we demonstrate the selflessness and humility that are at the core of our Christian Walk.

Engaging in outreach programs provides opportunities to connect with diverse individuals and communities, offering hope and support where it's most needed. Whether through volunteering at a local shelter, organizing food drives, or participating in global missions, our actions can create lasting impacts, transforming lives and communities. These experiences also remind us of our shared humanity, fostering empathy and understanding as we walk alongside those who are often marginalized or overlooked.

Furthermore, service and outreach empower us to witness the profound ways in which God works through us to bring about change. As we partner with others in these efforts, we strengthen our collective resolve to be agents of God's love and justice in the world. These endeavors also provide a platform for meaningful conversations about faith, allowing us to share the hope we have in Christ with those who may not yet know Him.

By prioritizing service and outreach, we cultivate a spirit of generosity and gratitude, keeping our hearts aligned with God's purposes. This outward focus not only enriches our spiritual journey but also reinforces our commitment to living a life that glorifies God. Through these acts of love and compassion, we become living testimonies of the gospel, inviting others to experience the joy and fulfillment that come from serving in His name.

5. Regular Reflection: Taking time for self-examination allows us to assess whether our actions and attitudes align with our faith. This practice helps to identify areas where we may be inadvertently drifting towards worldly ideologies.

Through regular reflection, we create a sacred space for introspection, where we can listen to the subtle nudges of the Holy Spirit guiding us back to the heart of our faith. This practice invites us to pause amidst the busyness of life, offering a moment of stillness to evaluate our spiritual journey honestly.

In these reflective moments, we can ask ourselves poignant questions: Are my actions and decisions rooted in love and truth? Am I prioritizing my relationship with God above the distractions and demands of the world? By engaging in this self-examination, we become more attuned to the ways in which worldly influences may have crept into our thoughts and behaviors, giving us the opportunity to recalibrate our lives according to God's will.

Moreover, reflection is not a solitary endeavor. Sharing our insights and struggles with trusted friends or mentors provides an added layer of accountability and encouragement. These relationships offer valuable perspectives and support as we seek to realign our lives with the teachings of Christ.

Regular reflection is a powerful tool in our spiritual toolkit, helping us to maintain clarity and purpose in our walk with God. By consistently assessing our hearts and minds, we ensure that our lives remain a testament to the transformative power of faith, shining as a light in the darkness and inspiring others to seek the enduring truth found in Christ.

Conclusion

A Personal Anecdote:

"After a particularly tense season, a young child asked me, 'Why don't my friends come to church anymore?' The question pierced deeper than any adult critique. Beneath the tension, children feel the chill of disunity. That little voice reminded me that division leaves spiritual orphans—and the cost is always higher than we admit."

The call to be in the world but not of it is a challenging yet essential aspect of our journey as followers of Christ. By being alert to the threat of worldliness and actively nurturing our distinct identity, we can shine brightly in a culture that desperately needs the hope and truth found in Jesus. Together, let us strive to embody the transformative power of the gospel, supporting one another in this crucial endeavor.

As we conclude, let us remember that our journey is not one of isolation, but of engagement. We are called to be salt and light, bringing flavor and illumination to a world yearning for meaning and direction. By faithfully committing to our spiritual disciplines, fostering authentic community, critically engaging with our culture, and serving others with compassion, we can navigate the challenges of worldliness with grace and integrity.

May our lives reflect the love and teachings of Christ, becoming beacons of hope and instruments of peace. As we walk this path together, let us encourage each other to remain steadfast, knowing that our efforts, no matter how small, contribute to the greater tapestry of God's work in the world. In this shared mission, we find purpose and fulfillment, living out our faith in ways that truly make a difference.

Chapter Five

Four-Alarm Fire
The Failure to Equip

A s fires can ignite from a lack of preparedness, so too does the spiritual landscape suffer from the Church's failure to adequately equip its members for the challenges of spiritual warfare. This chapter's purpose is to shine a bright light on the urgent need for discipleship, teaching, and serving within the body of Christ, as highlighted in **Ephesians 4:11-13**.

Anecdote:

"One Sunday, I felt the tug to preach a hard truth—one not wrapped in comfort, but conviction. I softened it. I hedged it. I

watched the congregation nod, but I saw no spark. That day, I learned something painful: silence doesn't always mean withholding words—it can mean withholding power. The pulpit had spoken, but heaven hadn't thundered."

In a world where the enemy prowls like a roaring lion, seeking to devour those who are unprepared, it is imperative that the Church takes its role seriously. The passage from Ephesians reminds us that Christ himself provides leaders for the purpose of equipping His people, so that they can effectively engage in spiritual battles.

Yet, too often, congregations find themselves ill-prepared, leaving their members vulnerable to doubt, confusion, and temptation. Without a concerted effort to invest in discipleship and spiritual formation, believers may falter when faced with the complexities of modern life and the subtle deceptions of the enemy.

To combat this, the Church must cultivate an environment where believers are not only taught but also empowered to teach others. This creates a ripple effect, where the knowledge and strength of one believer can influence and uplift an entire community. Leaders must encourage their congregations to delve deeper into their faith, asking questions and seeking answers together, thus building a robust foundation that can withstand any spiritual storm.

Furthermore, it is crucial for the Church to recognize and nurture the individual gifts and callings of each member. By doing so, the Church becomes a vibrant tapestry of diverse talents and abilities, all working in harmony to serve and support one another. When every believer is encouraged to step into their unique role, the Church can truly function as the body of Christ, unified and resilient.

This chapter serves as a clarion call for the Church to awaken to its responsibility. The time is now to equip every member with the tools and knowledge necessary to stand firm in their faith. Let us be proactive in fostering a community that is spiritually equipped, ready to face the challenges ahead with courage and conviction.

The Role of Discipleship

Discipleship is more than a program; it is the lifeblood of a thriving faith community. Each believer must take on the mantle of a disciple, not just to grow in knowledge but to actively pass that knowledge onto others. The Great Commission calls us to make disciples of all nations, but this starts at home, within our own circles. When we invest time in teaching biblical truths, we are not only nurturing our own faith but equipping others to navigate the complexities of life with a Christ-centered perspective.

It is through these intentional relationships that we see the transformative power of discipleship at work. Each interaction, each shared insight, becomes a building block in the spiritual house we are constructing together. This process is not confined to formal settings; it happens over coffee, during walks, and in the everyday moments that fill our lives.

As we engage in discipleship, we are reminded of the importance of humility and openness—qualities that allow us to learn from one another and to grow together. This mutual growth fosters a sense of accountability, where believers encourage and challenge each other to live out their faith authentically.

Moreover, discipleship is about cultivating a heart of compassion and service. As we learn and grow, we are called to extend our hands to those in need, using the wisdom and strength we have gained to lift others up. This is not merely an obligation but a joyous opportunity to reflect Christ's love in tangible ways.

In this dynamic process, the Church becomes a beacon of hope and a wellspring of strength, equipped to face any challenge with unity and purpose. Together, let us embrace the call to discipleship, recognizing it as both a privilege and a responsibility that empowers us to make a lasting impact in our communities and beyond.

The Importance of Teaching

Teaching is a critical component of equipping the saints. It is not enough to simply attend church on Sundays and absorb a sermon; engagement is required. Biblical teaching should challenge and inspire, prompting believers to seek a deeper understanding of Scripture. When we gather to learn, we create an environment in which questions are welcomed, discussions are encouraged, and faith is fortified.

Moreover, teaching should not be relegated to the pulpit. Every member of the congregation has a role to play, whether through leading small groups, mentoring younger believers, or providing resources for further study. When the Church embraces a culture of teaching and learning, every member becomes a lifeline of support for one another.

Through this collaborative pursuit of knowledge, the spiritual maturity of the entire community is nurtured, allowing each believer to flourish in their faith journey. This communal growth strengthens the bonds among members, creating a cohesive unit that is resilient in the face of adversity.

Teaching also serves as a bridge across generations, connecting the wisdom of those who have walked the path of faith for many years with the fresh perspectives of newer believers. This intergenerational exchange enriches the community, ensuring that the Church remains vibrant and relevant in an ever-changing world.

Furthermore, teaching equips believers to engage with the world outside the Church's walls. It empowers them to apply biblical principles to everyday situations, enabling them to be effective witnesses of Christ's love and truth in their workplaces, schools, and neighborhoods. As they gain confidence in their understanding of Scripture, believers are better prepared to discuss their faith with others, fostering meaningful conversations that can lead to transformation and healing.

Teaching is the catalyst for a living, breathing faith that is active and impactful. It is an ongoing journey of discovery, where believers are continually inspired to deepen their relationship with God and to share their insights with others. Through this commitment to teaching, the Church can truly fulfill its mission to equip every member for the work of the ministry, creating a community that is united in purpose and ready to face the challenges of the world with steadfast faith and unwavering hope.

A Personal Anecdote:

"I once scrapped an entire sermon at midnight. Something wasn't sitting right—not with the words, but with the Spirit. I began again, trembling, asking God for boldness. That next morning, I preached a message that burned through hesitation—and I saw tears, not just in the pews, but in hearts. That moment reminded me: truth must be spoken with trembling, not timidity."

The Call to Serve

Finally, serving is intertwined with equipping. Service is the natural outflow of a faith that is alive and active. As members of the body of Christ, we are called to use our unique gifts and talents for the benefit of others. Serving not only meets immediate needs but also fosters a sense of community and belonging, reminding us that we are not alone in our spiritual journey.

The fourth alarm alerts us to the spiritual fires that can easily spark when we fail to equip one another. It is a call to action—a reminder that the Church must actively engage in raising up warriors who are prepared to stand firm in their faith, grounded in the truth of God's Word.

To serve effectively, we must first be equipped with the knowledge and understanding of what it means to reflect Christ's love through our actions. Service is not merely an obligation; it is an expression of our faith and a testament to the transformative power of the Gospel. When we serve, we embody the teachings of Jesus, who exemplified humility and compassion in every interaction.

Service begins with a heart willing to listen and respond to the needs of others. It requires us to step beyond our comfort zones and to see each person as a valuable part of God's creation. Whether it is through acts of kindness, offering support to those in distress, or simply being present for someone in need, our service becomes a powerful witness to the world of the love and grace we have received.

Furthermore, serving together as a community strengthens the bonds between members, creating an environment where love and support flourish. It encourages each believer to step into their unique calling, using their gifts not for personal gain but for the collective growth and well-being of the Church. When we serve together, we become a living testament to the unity and diversity that can be found in the body of Christ.

Service is the culmination of discipleship and teaching. It is where our faith is put into action, where the lessons learned and the truths embraced are demonstrated through our lives. By embracing the call to serve, we not only fulfill our mission as followers of Christ but also inspire others to discover the joy and fulfillment that comes from giving of ourselves for the sake of others.

Let us, therefore, heed the fourth alarm and commit to equipping one another through discipleship, teaching, and service. In doing so, we will build a Church that is resilient, compassionate, and ready to shine brightly in a world that so desperately needs the light of Christ. Together, we can make a difference, one act of service at a time, as we stand firm in our faith and extend God's love to all.

The Church must address this failure to equip its members through intentional discipleship, comprehensive teaching, and an unwavering commitment to serve one another. By doing so, we can ensure that every believer is prepared to face the world's challenges, standing firm in the armor of God and ready to extinguish any flames that threaten to ignite. The time for action is now. Let us rise to the occasion and embrace the responsibility of equipping one another for the spiritual battles ahead.

A Personal Anecdote:

"After preaching on a controversial passage, one of our quietest members approached me and said, 'Pastor, thank you. I was beginning to wonder if anyone still believed the Word was enough.' Her eyes glistened—not with offense, but with relief. I realized then: silence in the pulpit breeds hunger in the pew. And when bold truth is spoken, people feast."

Together, as a unified body, we can transform our communities and beyond, becoming a beacon of hope and strength in a world that often seems dark and uncertain. Let us foster a culture of growth and empowerment, where every believer is encouraged to step into their God-given role with confidence and purpose.

This commitment to equipping each other will not only fortify our faith but also enable us to extend our reach, touching lives with the love of Christ in meaningful, impactful ways. As we invest in one another, we build a solid foundation that can withstand the challenges of the times, ensuring that the Church remains a vibrant and enduring testament to the Gospel's power and grace.

May we be inspired to continue this journey together, with hearts open to learning, serving, and leading others towards a deeper understanding of faith. Let us be the Church that rises to the call, ready to light the way forward with courage and conviction, always anchored in the truth and love of our Savior.

Sonnet for the Silence of the Pulpit

Charles E. Cracey

O pulpit veiled in velvet quiet's breath,
Where echoes die and prophecy lies still,
The Word grows pale beneath the fear of death,
And courage bends to comfort's fragile will.

No trumpet blasts, no clarion truth unfurled,
Just gentle hymns that never pierce the night.
The fire dimmed in corners of the world,
While watchmen sleep beneath the sacred light.

Yet silence is the loudest sin of all,
When heaven begs for voices steeped in flame.
Let tongues be kindled, let the righteous call—
Not for applause, but for the Lamb's acclaim.

Speak, preacher, speak! Let holy thunder roll,
And silence break beneath a burning soul.

Chapter Six

Five-Alarm Fire

Cultural Collapse and
Spiritual Slumber

A s the church stands on the precipice of a crisis, the metaphor of a five-alarm fire should evoke a sense of urgency and alarm among its leaders and congregants alike. Just as firefighters prepare to confront raging flames, so too must church leaders be ready to face the rising tide of false teachings and a drift away from core doctrines that have long sustained the faith.

A Personal Anecdote:

"I officiated a funeral where faith felt absent—not because the fam-

ily lacked love, but because hope had been replaced by sentiment. The room was heavy with legacy but light on eternity. I stood by the casket, praying for words, and the Spirit whispered: 'This is the cost when gospel fire cools.' That day, I realized our culture grieves deeply—but often without heaven's comfort."

The imagery of a five-alarm fire signals not just the immediacy of danger but also the comprehensive devastation it can cause if not contained swiftly and effectively. The moment we allow ambiguity to eclipse clarity on foundational beliefs, we risk our very identity as the Body of Christ. The Scriptures remind us in **2 Timothy 4:3** that "the time will come when people will not put up with sound doctrine." This reality is no longer a distant prophecy; it is a present-day crisis that demands our attention and action.

In this critical juncture, the church must marshal its resources and rally its members, much like a fire brigade assembling to combat a formidable blaze. It is time to reignite our commitment to doctrinal purity, ensuring that the teachings passed down through generations remain untarnished by the shifting sands of cultural trends.

By adopting a proactive stance, church leaders can create robust educational programs that delve deeply into Scripture, offering congregants a firm foundation upon which to build their faith. These programs should emphasize the importance of understanding both the letter and the spirit of biblical teachings, equipping believers with the tools needed to discern truth amidst the noise of modern-day interpretations.

Moreover, fostering a community that values open dialogue about faith-related challenges can serve as a bulwark against the encroaching tide of misinformation. Encouraging questions, exploring doubts, and seeking wisdom collectively will strengthen the bonds of fellowship and ensure that the church stands united in its mission to uphold the Gospel.

This five-alarm crisis is not merely a call to preserve the past, but an invitation to innovate and adapt, finding new ways to communicate timeless truths to a world in desperate need of hope. By embracing this challenge with courage and conviction, the church can emerge stronger, more resilient, and ready to shine the light of Christ into every corner of the world.

As we heed this urgent call, let us remember that we are not alone. The Holy Spirit guides us, providing wisdom and strength as we navigate the complexities of our time. Together, with faith as our compass and love as our guide, we can overcome the challenges before us and continue to build a church that reflects the beauty and truth of the Gospel for generations to come.

Leaders within the church are called to be vigilant guardians of the truth of the Gospel. This task is not merely about upholding tradition; it's about engaging in robust theological training and equipping themselves and their congregations to discern truth from error. As we delve into this chapter, we will explore the consequences of neglecting doctrinal integrity and the ways in which church leaders can fortify their communities against heretical influences.

The stakes are high, and the consequences of complacency profound. When leaders neglect doctrinal integrity, they risk allowing subtle distortions to take root, leading their congregations down paths that deviate from the essence of Christian teachings. This chapter will illuminate these dangers, drawing attention to historical examples where deviations have led to division and strife within the church, reminding us of the importance of remaining anchored in truth.

To combat these threats, church leaders must be proactive in building a solid foundation of knowledge and understanding. This involves fostering an environment where questioning and learning are encouraged, where the richness of Scripture is explored deeply, and where the history of the faith is not just recounted, but understood in its fullness. By doing so, congregants are empowered to navigate the complexities of modern-day interpretations that seek to dilute or distort the Gospel message.

A Personal Anecdote:

"A young entrepreneur once sat in my office, recently awarded, widely admired, and quietly undone. 'I have everything I ever prayed for,' he said, 'but it's like I lost myself in the getting.' His words echoed Psalm 127:1: 'Unless the Lord builds the house...' Success without spiritual anchor becomes a mirage. That conversation reminded me: cultural collapse doesn't begin in headlines—it starts in hearts starved of truth."

Furthermore, this chapter will highlight practical strategies for leaders to employ in their mission to safeguard their communities. From developing comprehensive educational programs to creating spaces for meaningful dialogue, these approaches serve as a bulwark against the encroachment of false teachings. By prioritizing theological literacy and encouraging active participation from all members, the church can cultivate a resilient faith community capable of withstanding external pressures.

Through stories of perseverance and faithfulness, we will see how churches that have prioritized doctrinal integrity have not only survived but thrived, becoming beacons of hope and truth in their communities. As we continue this exploration, let us be inspired to take up the mantle of vigilance, ensuring that the light of the Gospel remains undimmed for generations to come.

One crucial aspect of safeguarding the faith is fostering a culture of theological literacy. Just as firefighters train tirelessly to respond to emergencies, so too must church leaders be diligent in their study of Scripture and church history. This means understanding not only the tenets of their faith but also the historical context in which these doctrines developed. Engaging with hermeneutics, the science of interpretation, is imperative in equipping believers to discern the subtleties of modern teachings that might lead them astray.

By delving into the rich historical tapestry of the church, leaders can draw wisdom from the past, learning from both triumphs and trials. This comprehensive approach enables them to better address contemporary challenges with a well-rounded perspective.

Moreover, creating opportunities for congregants to engage in theological study can ignite a passion for learning and spiritual growth. Bible study groups, workshops, and seminars can serve as platforms for believers to deepen their understanding and develop critical thinking skills. Encouraging participation in these activities helps to build a resilient community that is not easily swayed by misleading doctrines.

In addition to formal education, nurturing a culture where theological discussion is a regular part of church life is essential. Informal gatherings, such as coffee discussions or after-service chats, offer spaces for members to explore questions and share insights, fostering a sense of unity and mutual support.

The goal is to cultivate a congregation that is not only informed but also inspired to live out their faith with conviction. As believers grow in their knowledge and understanding, they become more effective ambassadors of the Gospel, shining brightly in a world that desperately needs truth and hope. Through this commitment to theological literacy, the church can stand firm against the shifting sands of cultural trends, ensuring that the light of the Gospel remains a beacon for all to see.

Furthermore, leaders must cultivate an environment where questions and doubts are met with open dialogue and scriptural grounding. A healthy church community encourages its members to seek deeper understanding and wrestle with challenging theological concepts rather than shying away from them. This engagement can fortify believers against the allure of trendy doctrines that cater to personal preferences rather than scriptural truths.

By fostering an atmosphere where inquiry is welcomed and valued, congregants can grow in their faith and build resilience against the shifting ideologies of the modern world. This process of questioning and exploration should be anchored in love and respect, creating a safe space for individuals to express their uncertainties and seek guidance from more seasoned members of the faith community.

To support this, church leaders might consider implementing regular forums or discussion groups that focus on complex theological issues or current events viewed through a biblical lens. These gatherings can serve as a means for believers to come together, share diverse perspectives, and deepen their collective understanding of faith matters. By doing so, the church becomes a vibrant learning community where everyone, regardless of their stage in faith, feels valued and heard.

Moreover, mentorship programs can be established to pair newer believers with those who have walked longer in their faith journey. This one-on-one interaction not only provides personalized support but also builds intergenerational relationships that enrich the entire congregation. Through these connections, wisdom and encouragement are passed down, helping to sustain a robust faith community.

In addition to structured programs, church leaders should encourage a culture of lifelong learning, where personal study and engagement with Scripture are part of everyday life. Encouraging the use of devotional materials, online resources, and theological literature can inspire individuals to delve deeper into their faith outside of formal settings. This personal pursuit of knowledge ensures that believers are continually growing and ready to face the challenges that arise in their spiritual walk.

By creating a church environment that values both questioning and learning, leaders empower their congregations to stand firm in their beliefs, equipped with a solid foundation of biblical truth. This not only strengthens individual faith but also cultivates a community that is united in purpose and ready to share the transformative message of the Gospel with the world.

As we navigate this crisis of faith, we must also confront the apathy that sometimes infiltrates our congregations. Like a slow-burning ember that can ignite a fire, indifference towards sound doctrine can ultimately lead to spiritual disarray. It is imperative that church leaders ignite a passion for biblical truth within their flocks—a passion that will withstand the flames of cultural shifts and societal pressures.

This begins with cultivating an environment where enthusiasm for learning and living out the Gospel is both encouraged and celebrated. Leaders can inspire this passion by modeling a genuine love for Scripture and demonstrating how its teachings apply to everyday life. Engaging sermons, interactive Bible studies, and personal testimonies can all serve as catalysts for spiritual awakening and growth.

Moreover, fostering a sense of community and belonging plays a crucial role in combating apathy. When congregants feel connected to one another, they are more likely to engage actively in their faith journey. Church gatherings should be infused with warmth and fellowship, creating spaces where individuals feel supported and valued. By doing so, leaders can transform their churches into vibrant communities that prioritize spiritual vitality over complacency.

Additionally, empowering lay leaders to take active roles in ministry can help reignite passion within the congregation. By involving members in teaching, outreach, and service, the church not only distributes the responsibility of spiritual care but also encourages personal ownership of faith development. This collaborative approach can lead to a more dynamic and resilient church body.

Ultimately, addressing apathy requires intentional efforts to awaken hearts and minds to the beauty and relevance of the Gospel. Through committed leadership and a nurturing community, the church can become a beacon of hope and truth, standing firm against the tide of indifference and inspiring a renewed dedication to faith in every member.

Finally, we must remember that theological training is not an exclusive endeavor for pastors and scholars. Every member of the congregation has a role to play in preserving the integrity of the Gospel. By fostering a sense of ownership over their faith, believers are empowered to defend it against distortions that seek to undermine its core. This collective responsibility means that each individual is equipped to be a guardian of truth, standing firm in their convictions and ready to share the hope of the Gospel with those around them.

To achieve this, churches can encourage personal study and engagement through accessible resources and diverse learning opportunities. Whether through small group discussions, online courses, or reading plans, these tools can help believers deepen their understanding and grow in their faith journey.

Moreover, integrating faith into everyday life is essential. Encouraging believers to live out their beliefs in their workplaces, schools, and communities not only strengthens their personal faith but also serves as a witness to others. This holistic approach ensures that the light of the Gospel shines brightly in every aspect of life, creating ripples of positive influence.

As we move forward, let us commit to nurturing an environment where theological literacy and active faith go hand in hand, empowering every believer to serve as a steward of the Gospel's truth and love. Together, we can build a resilient and vibrant community that stands unwavering in the face of challenges, ready to illuminate the world with the enduring message of Christ.

In conclusion, a five-alarm crisis of faith necessitates immediate, focused action. The church must rise to the occasion, championing sound doctrine and engaging in robust theological training to protect believers from the dangers that threaten their faith. As leaders, we are entrusted with the sacred duty to safeguard the truth of the Gospel—a responsibility that we must approach with the same urgency and resolve as those who confront the fiercest of fires. The stability and health of our faith communities depend on it, and it is our calling to ensure that the light of truth continues to shine brightly amidst the darkness.

With unwavering dedication, we must foster environments where faith is not only preserved but also actively nurtured. This involves creating spaces that encourage growth, questioning, and exploration, ensuring that believers are well-equipped to navigate the complexities of modern life while remaining anchored in biblical truth.

By investing in comprehensive educational programs and promoting open dialogue, we empower individuals to deepen their understanding and commitment to their faith. This proactive approach helps to fortify our communities against the encroachment of misleading teachings and cultural pressures, ensuring that the Gospel remains a guiding beacon.

Moreover, as we engage in this critical work, let us remember the power of unity and collaboration. By joining forces across generations and denominations, we can share resources, wisdom, and encouragement, building a resilient network of believers steadfast in their mission. Together, we can cultivate a vibrant faith community that not only withstands external challenges but also thrives, offering hope and truth to a world in need.

In this endeavor, let us draw strength from the Holy Spirit, who guides and empowers us in our pursuit of truth. As we continue to champion sound doctrine and foster theological literacy, we fulfill our calling to preserve the integrity of the Gospel for future generations. Let us move forward with courage and conviction, confident in the transformative power of faith to illuminate even the darkest corners of the world.

Conclusion: Sounding the Alarm for Renewal

In this pivotal moment, we stand at a crossroads, faced with alarms that beckon us to renewal. The time has come for the Church to awaken from its slumber and confront the pressing issues that threaten to engulf our communities and our mission. This is not merely a call to awareness, but a rallying cry urging believers to unite in prayer, action, and restoration.

As we look to the future, we can envision a vibrant and effective witness for Christ—one that can illuminate the darkness and bring hope to a world yearning for truth and love. Our roadmap for renewal is clear: it begins with heartfelt prayer, seeking divine guidance to address our shortcomings and to inspire bold initiatives that reflect the heart of God.

Through fervent prayer, we open ourselves to the transformative power of the Holy Spirit, inviting His wisdom to guide our decisions and actions. This spiritual awakening must be accompanied by tangible efforts to engage with our communities, meeting their physical and spiritual needs with compassion and grace. By embodying Christ's love in practical ways, we demonstrate the Gospel's relevance and draw others into the warmth of His embrace.

Moreover, as we strive for renewal, let us cultivate an atmosphere of inclusivity and grace within our congregations. By embracing diversity and fostering unity, we reflect the kingdom of God, where every individual is valued and every voice is heard. This requires intentional efforts to break down barriers and build bridges, ensuring that all feel welcome and cherished in our midst.

Education and discipleship remain central to this renewal process. We must invest in equipping believers with the knowledge and tools they need to live out their faith confidently and effectively. This includes not only theological training but also practical skills for ministry and service. By empowering individuals to take ownership of their faith journey, we create a dynamic and engaged community ready to tackle the challenges of our time.

Finally, let us not forget the power of testimony. Sharing stories of transformation and hope can inspire others to seek their own encounters with God. As we witness to the work of Christ in our lives, we become beacons of His light, illuminating the path for others to follow.

In embracing this call to renewal, we commit to being agents of change, dedicated to advancing God's kingdom on earth. Together, through prayer, action, and a spirit of unity, we can ignite a revival that not only revitalizes our churches but also transforms the world around us, making it a reflection of God's love and glory.

Next, we must embrace action, stepping out in faith to meet the needs of those around us. This could take the form of outreach programs, community service, and advocating for justice—all rooted in the teachings of Christ.

By actively engaging with the needs of our communities, we embody the compassion and love that Jesus modeled throughout His ministry. Outreach programs can serve as lifelines, connecting individuals with resources and support that address both immediate and long-term needs. Whether it's organizing food drives, offering educational workshops, or providing shelter for those in crisis, each act of service becomes a tangible expression of our faith and commitment to the Gospel.

Community service, in its many forms, not only reflects Christ's love but also strengthens the bonds within our congregations. As we work side by side, we learn from one another, growing in empathy and understanding. These shared experiences foster a sense of unity and purpose, reminding us that we are all part of a larger mission to bring light to a world in need.

Advocating for justice, meanwhile, aligns our actions with the heart of God, who calls us to "act justly, love mercy, and walk humbly" with Him (Micah 6:8). This might involve standing against discrimination, supporting initiatives that promote equality, or lending our voices to causes that uplift the marginalized. In doing so, we not only address systemic issues but also demonstrate the transformative power of the Gospel to effect change.

As we step out in faith, let us remember that these actions are not merely obligations but opportunities to share the love of Christ with others. Each encounter is a chance to sow seeds of hope and to witness the Spirit at work, drawing people closer to the truth and grace of God.

In this pursuit, let us rely on the strength and guidance of the Holy Spirit, trusting that He equips us for every good work. With hearts open to His leading, we can navigate the challenges of our time with courage and compassion, confident that our efforts can spark lasting change in the lives we touch. Together, through purposeful action and unwavering faith, we can build a future that reflects the beauty and justice of God's kingdom on earth.

Finally, we invite believers to a season of restoration, where reconciliation with one another and a recommitment to our mission can breathe new life into the Church. It is through this collective response that we can fulfill our calling and emerge as beacons of hope in a tumultuous world.

Let us heed the alarms that sound around us, not with despair, but with a renewed spirit of purpose and determination. Together, we can foster a revival that reflects the love and grace of our Savior—transforming lives and communities for His glory.

As we embark on this journey of restoration, we must embrace the opportunity to rebuild and strengthen the bonds within our faith communities. This begins with an intentional focus on reconciliation, where open communication and forgiveness pave the way for healing. By addressing past hurts and misunderstandings, we can create a foundation of trust and unity that empowers us to move forward with a shared vision.

In this season, let us also recommit to our mission, reminding ourselves and each other of the core values and principles that define us as followers of Christ. This recommitment involves both personal reflection and communal affirmation, ensuring that every member feels connected to the larger purpose of the Church. Through prayer, worship, and collective discernment, we can align our efforts with the divine calling placed upon us.

Moreover, as we restore and renew, let us be mindful of the transformative power of service. By reaching out to those in need, both within and beyond our congregations, we demonstrate the heart of Christ in tangible ways. This service is not just an act of charity, but a profound expression of the Gospel, inviting others to experience the love and hope that we have found.

A Personal Anecdote:

"I once woke up hours before a revival meeting—heart heavy, Spirit stirring. The message I had planned didn't fit the moment. I kneeled by my desk, praying through tears: 'Lord, don't let this be a gathering. Let it be ignition.' That night, something happened. Not flashy, not loud—but holy. People lingered. Children prayed. Elders embraced strangers. The slumber cracked. Fire flickered again."

As we work towards these goals, let us be guided by the Holy Spirit, who breathes life into our endeavors and fills us with the courage to face the challenges ahead. With faith as our foundation and love as our guide, we can navigate this season of restoration with grace and resilience, knowing that our efforts will bear fruit for generations to come.

Together, let us be the Church—a vibrant, compassionate, and unwavering presence in a world that is often fraught with uncertainty. By nurturing a spirit of renewal, we can illuminate the path forward, inspiring others to join us in the transformative journey of faith. Through this collective response, we fulfill our calling to be beacons of hope, shining brightly in the midst of a tumultuous world and pointing others to the eternal light of Christ.

SONNET FOR A FIVE-ALARM FIRE

Charles E. Cravey

In times of crisis, let the bells resound,
A five-alarm that calls us to the fight.
To stand on holy ground where truth is found,
And shine the Gospel's ever-radiant light.

With hearts ablaze, we rally to the cause,
Against the tides that seek to blur the line.
To guard the ancient truth, our fervent laws,
Ensuring faith remains a beacon fine.

Oh, let us not be swayed by fleeting trends,
Nor wander from the path that leads to grace.

In unity, our steadfast love extends,
To all who seek a haven in this space.

Together, let us rise with purpose clear,
A Church renewed, where hope is ever near.

Chapter Seven

Fanning the Flame of Revival

A **Personal Anecdote:**
"Years ago, I mentored a young preacher fresh from seminary. His eyes sparkled with fire, but his voice trembled with inexperience. After his first sermon, he sat beside me, anxious. 'Did it matter?' he asked. I replied, 'You spoke truth, and that always matters.' Watching him grow reignited something in me—not ambition, but awe. Revival isn't always loud—it's often whispered from one soul to the next."

We've walked through the smoldering realities of spiritual lethargy, complacency, division, and despair. Yet through these trials, the fire in the pulpit can be rekindled—not as a spectacle, but as a beacon.

Revival begins not in policy but in posture. It's in the quiet prayers before dawn, in elders listening to youth, in pulpits that preach Christ with tears and truth. The five alarms aren't merely stages—they're signals. Signals that something sacred is stirring.

Let this final chapter be a commissioning. To the preacher: Speak with boldness, tempered in humility. To the worshiper: Come as firewood—ready to be lit. To the seeker: You are welcome in the warmth.

A Personal Anecdote:

"After a passionate message on spiritual awakening, an elder leaned over and said quietly, 'We haven't seen this fire in years, Pastor. Thank you for bringing it back.' Her words weren't flattery—they were a marker. A signal that the embers weren't dead, just buried. That moment reminded me that revival often comes

not in declarations, but in recognition. When a weary heart begins to warm again."

The pulpit's fire, when properly tended, spills into pews, homes, and hearts. It is not ours to control but to honor. Let us go forth, not merely warmed, but ignited—carrying revival into the world with reverent joy.

Anecdote:

"One evening, I gathered a stack of old sermon manuscripts—dozens of outlines that once stirred rooms but had since become relics. I placed them in a hearth and let them burn. Not out of frustration, but renewal. 'Lord,' I prayed, 'let tomorrow's fire not be borrowed, but born anew.' That surrender marked a turning point for me. I stopped chasing old sparks—and started seeking fresh flame."

Devotional Reflection: "Tending the Holy Flame"

Lord of the Burning Bush,

You have sounded the alarms—and we have heard them. Not

with fear, but with faith. Not with panic, but with purpose. You are a consuming fire, yet you refine rather than destroy.

Kindle within us a pulpit that speaks truth with trembling lips. Kindle within our hearts a worship that does not flicker with emotion but blazes with conviction. Remind us that revival is not born in spectacle, but in surrender.

Let us not simply watch the fire—we ask to become it. Holy flame of heaven, fall on Your church. Burn away our complacency, illuminate our calling, and empower our witness.

Let our lives become embers of Your glory,

Our prayers, the sparks of transformation,

Our pulpits are the hearth of a rising generation.

This is not the end. This is the ignition.

Amen.

FOR MORE BOOKS BY DR. CHARLES E. CRAVEY:

https://drcharlescravey.com or

Amazon.com/CharlesCraveyBooks